NEW VANGUARD • 156

KRIEGSMARINE AUXILIARY CRUISERS

GORDON WILLIAMSON   ILLUSTRATED BY IAN PALMER

First published in Great Britain in 2009 by Osprey Publishing,
Midland House, West Way, Botley, Oxford OX2 0PH, UK
44-02 23rd St, Suite 219, Long Island City, NY 11101, USA
Email: info@ospreypublishing.com

A CIP catalogue record for this book is available from the British Library

Print ISBN: 978 1 84603 333 9
PDF e-book ISBN: 978 1 84603 881 5

Page layouts by Melissa Orrom Swan, Oxford
Typeset in Sabon and Myraid Pro
Index by Alan Thatcher
Originated by PPS Grasmere Ltd., Leeds
Printed in China through World Print Ltd.

10 11 12 13 14   11 10 9 8 7 6 5 4 3 2

FOR A CATALOGUE OF ALL BOOKS PUBLISHED BY OSPREY MILITARY
AND AVIATION PLEASE CONTACT:

Osprey Direct, c/o Random House Distribution Center,
400 Hahn Road, Westminster, MD 21157
E-mail: uscustomerservice@ospreypublishing.com

Osprey Direct, The Book Service Ltd, Distribution Centre,
Colchester Road, Frating Green, Colchester, Essex, CO7 7DW
E-mail: customerservice@ospreypublishing.com

www.ospreypublishing.com

Osprey Publishing is supporting the Woodland Trust, the UK's leading
woodland conservation charity, by funding the dedication of trees.

EDITOR'S NOTE

For ease of comparison between types, metric measurements are used
almost exclusively throughout this book. The following data will help
in converting metric to imperial measurements:

1 kilometre = 0.6 mile

1 mile = 1.6km

1 metre = 3.28ft (1.09 yards)

1kg = 2.2lbs

1 tonne = 0.98 Imp tons

1 litre = 0.2 Imp gal = 0.18 US gal

1 Imp gal = 4.5 litres

1hp = 0.745kW

CONTENTS

KRIEGSMARINE AUXILIARY CRUISERS

INTRODUCTION

Although German capital ships like the *Bismarck* could and did take on enemy warships of similar size, the intended role of the larger Kriegsmarine vessels – the 'pocket battleships', battleships and heavy cruisers – had always been commerce-raiding. Although a minor degree of success was achieved by some of the larger warships in attacks on Allied merchant shipping, the auxiliary cruisers – relatively unknown when compared to famous vessels like *Admiral Graf Spee*, or indeed when compared to the most famous of all German warship types, the U-boats – proved to be, in comparative terms, immensely successful. This success could be measured not only in terms of the tonnage of Allied shipping that they sank, but also in the number of Allied warships that were diverted from other missions to try to track them down.

The Royal Navy also used 'auxiliary cruisers', but the British term tended to be applied to merchant vessels that had been openly fitted with a few medium-calibre guns in order to protect convoys from attack. The German auxiliary cruisers, though also starting life as merchantmen, were very heavily armed, usually carrying torpedo tubes as well as guns and sometimes even their own aircraft – and their weapons were carefully concealed. Far from being tasked simply with protecting other merchantmen, these ships were aggressive predators, searching the sea-lanes for unsuspecting Allied vessels which would not suspect their true nature until it was too late. (It is worth

One of the Great War forerunners of the Kriegsmarine's auxiliary cruisers, the *Prinz Eitel Friedrich* is shown here tied up at the Philadelphia Navy Yard after her surrender in 1917. She sank a total of 11 Allied ships in both the Pacific and South Atlantic Oceans. (Naval Historical Center)

noting that many of the Allied crews that fell foul of these raiders, removed from their ships before they were sunk or sent back to Germany as prizes, commented on the decent treatment they received while held prisoner.) These powerful ships were capable not only of destroying merchant ships but, in extremis, of defending themselves against well armed enemy warships; in the most famous of such encounters, the heavy cruiser HMAS *Sydney* was sunk in battle by the *Hilfskreuzer Kormoran*.

A total of 11 ships were converted into auxiliary cruisers, usually in great secrecy; and although their designations were simply a blandly anonymous number such as 'Schiff 16', they quickly became better known by their more evocative names – *Atlantis, Kormoran, Thor, Komet* and the rest. This book describes the specifications and armament of the auxiliary cruisers, as well as summarizing their combat histories and their eventual fates.

* * *

The Kriegsmarine's use of auxiliary cruisers should not have come as any surprise to the Allies, since the Kaiserliche Marine had employed such Hilfskreuzere widely during the Great War. A number of these had achieved fame, when converted merchant vessels such as the *Berlin, Kronprinz Wilhelm, Möwe, Prinz Eitel Friedrich* and *Wolf II* between them took a heavy toll of Allied shipping. The auxiliary cruisers of the Kaiser's navy ranged from sailing ships through merchantmen to large ocean liners, but experience proved that those which showed most promise were the converted merchantmen. Although they lacked the speed of the ocean liners, the smaller merchantmen made less obvious targets for enemy warships and had much lower fuel requirements.

Between them, nine of the auxiliary cruisers of the World War II Kriegsmarine sank or captured a total of 129 vessels, representing some 780,000 tons of shipping. This achievement, by a total of around 3,400 officers and men – the total who served aboard the auxiliary cruisers – represented incredible value. The cost of refurbishing the entire fleet of former merchantmen, generally outfitted with older, surplus weaponry, was only around one per cent of the cost of constructing a single major warship such as *Bismarck* or *Tirpitz*.

None of these auxiliary cruisers could possibly be described as aesthetically attractive, but that was a positive point in their favour. They were intended to look anonymous and unthreatening until the moment when the Reichskriegsflagge was run up at the mast, the guns were cleared for action, and the destructive potential of a powerful warship was unleashed against the shocked victim. Despite the great successes they would achieve, the auxiliary cruisers were not initially considered as particularly important. They were crewed by volunteers who could be spared from other branches, and commanded by officers – usually from the Reserves – not considered dashing and aggressive enough to be given command of modern warships.

Significantly, the seamen and their ships were considered expendable. Nevertheless, these crews earned such respect during the first 18 months of the war that Grossadmiral Raeder (commander-in-chief of the Kriegsmarine at the outbreak of war and until January 1943) recognized their contribution to the war effort by authorizing a special War Badge. Instituted on 24 April 1941,

The Auxiliary Cruiser War Badge in yellow and white metal finish, designed by the Berlin artist Wilhelm Ernst Peekhaus. The image of a Norse longship, surmounting the globe and heading into the North Atlantic, speaks for itself. (Author's collection)

ABOVE

A rare example of an award document for the Auxiliary Cruiser War Badge, to a crew member of the *Orion*. As was normal with the documents for this badge, it is signed by the ship's captain – in this case Kurt Weyher. (Author's collection)

ABOVE RIGHT

A Matrosenobergefreiter of the signals branch proudly wears the Auxiliary Cruiser War Badge in the regulation position on the left breast of his jumper. Since such war badges were awards rather than insignia, they would continue to be worn even if the sailor transferred to another branch of the Navy. (Deutsches U-Boot Museum)

the *Hilfskreuzer Kriegsabzeichen* was designed by Wilhelm Ernst Peekhaus; it consisted of a vertical oval wreath of oakleaves topped by an eagle and swastika with wings outspread. In the centre of the badge was the top part of a globe of the world showing the North Atlantic, surmounted by a three-quarter-front view of a Viking longship, harking back to the sea raiders of an earlier age. The wreath, eagle and longship were in gold finish, with the globe in toned silver.

It is interesting to note that a number of examples of this badge were manufactured in Japan on behalf of the Germans, for award to crews of auxiliary cruisers operating in the Pacific who, due to the distance from home, were unable to obtain the official award pieces. A further and very elaborate version of the badge was created on the authority of Grossadmiral Raeder for award to the most successful auxiliary cruiser commanders. Not an official award, but rather a personal gift from the C-in-C Navy, this badge was in solid silver and gilt, and had the swastika set with small rose-cut diamonds. In fact only one example of this badge was ever presented, to Kapitän zur See Bernhard Rogge, commander of the raider *Atlantis*.

Terminology

Printed sources refer to each of the auxiliary cruisers in a number of ways. Firstly, each was given an official mumber with the prefix HSK, running in chronological sequence. Officially this was the abbreviation for Handelsschutzkreuzer, 'trade protection cruiser', but the term Hilfskreuzer, 'auxiliary cruiser', was more common and was used in the official title of the War Badge. Secondly, each was given a coded ship number (e.g. Schiff 36); each captain gave his ship a name; and finally, each was given a code letter by the Allies (e.g. Raider A).

Thus, for example, HSK 2 *Atlantis* was referred to officially as Schiff 16, and was known to the Allies as Raider C. In the text which follows the 11 vessels whose conversion to this role was completed or begun are listed by name, in order of their actual or potential HSK pennant numbers.

THE CRUISERS

ORION
HSK 1; Schiff 36; Raider A

Specification:

Built	Blohm & Voss, Hamburg	Powerplant	2x Blohm & Voss turbines
Launched	1930	Top speed	15 knots
Original name	*Kurmark*	Endurance	35,000 nautical miles
Length	148m	Armament	6x 15cm guns, 1x 7.5cm, 2x 3.7cm flak, 4x 2cm flak; 6x torpedo tubes; up to 230 mines; 2x Arado Ar196 floatplanes
Beam	18.6m		
Displacement	7,020 tons	Crew	376

Operational history

One of the first vessels to undergo conversion to the auxiliary cruiser role, the merchant ship *Kurmark* began refitting as a warship at the Blohm & Voss yards in Hamburg in the spring of 1939, emerging in December of that year as HSK 1. She was commissioned into the Kriegsmarine under Kapitän zur See Kurt Weyher. The next three months were spent training and working up in the Baltic before, in March 1940, she made her way through the Kattegat and Skagerrak into the North Sea. She paused for a few days after passing Cuxhaven in order for her grey military livery to be repainted to take on her first disguise, as the Dutch freighter *Beemsterdijk*.

Eventually, on 6 April 1940, Weyher received his sailing orders and headed north, up the coast of Norway before making the long hook west around the northernmost British Isles and Iceland, then south again through the Denmark Strait between Iceland and Greenland. His first real test came two days later when the raider was approached by two British destroyers.

Dusk falls, and HSK 1 *Orion* is silhouetted against the horizon, looking for all the world like an innocent merchantman. (Deutsches U-Boot Museum)

7

A view looking towards the stern of *Orion*. In the centre can be seen one of the main gun turrets; note that it is trained inboard and forward, so that from a distance the turret will appear like a small deckhouse and its barrel like a small spar attached to the mast. (Deutsches U-Boot Museum)

The disguise passed the test, and the British warships accepted her as the Dutch freighter she purported to be. Before attempting the Denmark Strait the captain then changed his disguise twice more in a couple of weeks, first posing as the Soviet ship *Sovtorgflot* and then, on entering waters where a Soviet merchantman would be unlikely to be seen, HSK 1 became the Greek freighter *Rokos*.

Weyher was ordered to pause briefly to attack shipping in the Atlantic before proceeding to the Indian Ocean, in order to cause confusion and persuade the Allies that a major German warship was operating in the area. On 24 April the opportunity came for *Orion* to prove herself, when she encountered a British armed freighter. Running up the German flag, Weyher crossed the other ship's bows and ordered her to stop; when she did not, and began sending the raider warning signal 'R-R-R', Weyher opened fire. The British ship was no match for the *Orion*, and was soon blazing as her crew prepared to abandon ship. On picking up the survivors and recovering a number of bodies of those killed in the action, Weyher learned that the first victim of the auxiliary cruiser fleet was the 5,200-ton freighter *Haxby*. Once clear of the area, Weyher paraded his crew and buried the Allied dead at sea with full honours.

Australian waters and the Pacific

On 1 May, *Orion* crossed the Equator, now posing as the Brazilian *Lloyd Brasiliero*; on 13 May she rendezvoused with the tanker *Winnetou* and refuelled. *Orion* rounded Cape Horn on May 21, and was ordered to hunt for enemy shipping off the coast of Australia. Disguised now as an anonymous Dutch freighter, the raider reached her target area on 12 June, but only after forcing her way through heavy seas and suffering engine problems. Her first operation was to lay more than 200 mines in the approaches to the Hauraki Gulf near Auckland, New Zealand, after which Capt Weyher made plans to meet up with the *Winnetou* to refuel once again.

Weyher's mines scored an early success when the liner *Niagra* hit one en route to Canada, and went down carrying a load of small arms ammunition and more than 8 tons of gold bullion belonging to the Bank of England.

At something of a disadvantage in spotting fresh targets due to the loss of his Arado floatplane when it capsized in heavy seas, Weyher had some good fortune when his lookouts spotted the lights of a ship heading his way. Waiting until after the ship had passed astern, Weyher ran up his battle ensign and ordered her to stop. A full salvo fired to land just short of her had the desired effect, and the Norwegian *Tropic Sea*, carrying a cargo of wheat for Britain, surrendered immediately. Rather than sink the freighter Weyher took her as a prize, and both ships then met up with *Winnetou* on 25 June for refuelling.

Weyher spent the next few weeks searching in vain for new targets; he made rendezvous with *Winnetou* to refuel on 1 July and again on 7 August. Finally, after many weeks of fruitless searching, Weyher spotted an Allied ship on 10 August, but the *Triona* proved the faster and evaded the raider. Weyher then took *Orion* into the waters off New Caledonia, where on 16 August he intercepted the collier *Notou* with a full load of British coal; she surrendered after a warning shot was fired. Her crew were evacuated and their ship sent to the bottom with a mixture of demolition charges and gunfire.

Orion now moved to the Tasman Sea, which was intended to be her last hunting ground before returning home via the Indian Ocean. Here Weyher intercepted the freighter *Turakina* which, far from surrendering, returned

A rare overhead view of *Orion*, during her trials in the winter of 1939–40, shown here in an icy harbour with a tugboat alongside. The aft funnel was removed shortly before she set off on her first operational cruise. Just visible at bottom centre is a gun turret concealed by hinged panels on the hull side, which could be folded down. The stern turret is also visible in this view. (Deutsches U-Boot Museum)

fire, sent out radio warning signals and tried to escape. After a pursuit the raider's overwhelming superiority in firepower soon saw the *Turakina* reduced to a blazing wreck. Realising she was finished, Weyher ordered his gunners to cease fire and approached the stricken enemy to pick up survivors. Incredibly, the *Turakina* then opened fire again, prompting a furious Weyher to reply with a full broadside from both his primary and secondary armament. Once again displaying considerable chivalry, and despite knowing that alerted Allied warships might be heading for the area, Weyher took the time to drop dinghies overboard on tow ropes, and managed to rescue a number of survivors.

Orion then left the area, and despite being spotted twice by Allied aircraft was able to maintain her disguise as a harmless merchantman. She headed for the Marshall Islands for a rendezvous with the supply ship *Regensburg*, and in these waters Weyher decided to disguise his ship as a Japanese freighter. However, it transpired that no one aboard had any knowledge of Japanese kanji characters, so some random lettering was chosen from the wrapping of a roll of film, and this was painted on the hull. *Orion* then proceeded to her rendezvous with her flanks emblazoned with the legend 'Not suitable for use in the tropics'.

After the resupply rendezvous *Orion* and *Regensburg* both sailed towards a meeting with Capt Robert Eyssen's auxiliary cruiser *Komet*. On 14 October 1940 the raider intercepted the Norwegian freighter *Ringwood*, which surrendered without a struggle. The latest prize had no cargo and *Orion* had no spare fuel to send her home as a prize, so she was sunk with demolition charges. *Orion* did benefit, however, from the acquisition of the *Ringwood*'s ship's cat, which did wonders in keeping down the rats that infested the raider. On 18 October *Orion* and *Regensburg* finally met up with *Komet* and the tanker *Kulmerland* at Lamotrek Atoll in the Caroline Islands.

All of the German ships were disguised as Japanese merchantmen; unfortunately, two of them were posing as the same ship. The following day a real Japanese liner appeared on the scene and saw through the ruse, but the Germans were able to persuade the Japanese that they were simply harmless merchantmen using the Japanese disguise to protect themselves from Allied warships.

With *Orion* and *Komet* now operating in conjunction, on 25 November the German force intercepted the freighter *Holmwood*; as well as carrying a few civilian passengers she had more than 1,300 sheep on board, providing the raider crews with a source of fresh meat. Two days later *Orion*'s lookouts spotted a sizeable vessel running without lights. Flanked by *Komet* and *Orion*, the large New Zealand passenger ship *Rangitane* immediately sent a distress signal, but was forced to halt after being battered by gunfire from *Komet*. She was relatively heavily armed, and her captain's decision to surrender was no doubt influenced by her carrying more than 100 civilian passengers including many women. She was also carrying a considerable load of frozen meat and dairy products, but the need to escape before Allied warships arrived meant that there was only time to evacuate the passengers and crew and not to recover any of the cargo.

The two raiders scored their next victory on 6 December 1940 when they intercepted and sank the British freighter *Triona*, but this time *Orion* was able to recover both the survivors and the cargo of foodstsuffs. On the following day, while en route with *Komet* to carry out an attack on Nauru, west of the Gilbert Islands, the *Orion* intercepted and sank two British freighters, the *Triadic* and the *Triaster*. After this action *Orion* sailed back to Lamotrek Atoll, where her engines were overhauled and fresh fuel and supplies taken on board. On 6 January 1941, Capt Weyher departed Lamotrek after being informed that his location might have been compromised, and moved to the Japanese-occupied island of Muag, where repairs continued until the end of the month. Just before her departure on 6 February, *Orion* completed her re-supply operation and was also provided with a floatplane purchased from the Japanese to replace her wrecked Arado.

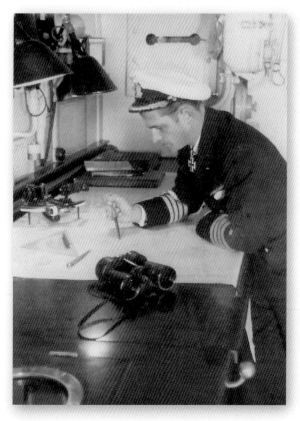

The *Orion's* commander, Kapitän zur See Kurt Weyher, posed as if studying his charts. Note the Knight's Cross of the Iron Cross worn at his throat, dating the photo to no earlier than 24 August 1941. (Deutsches U-Boot Museum)

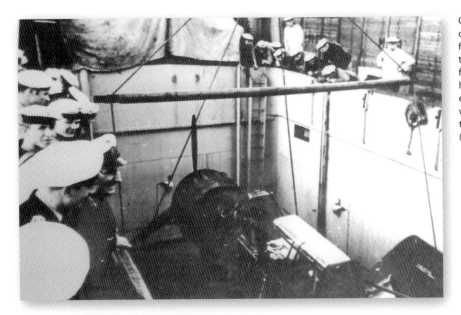

Crew members watch as one of the *Orion*'s Arado Ar196 floatplanes is lowered into the hold. Even with its wings folded it was a tight fit, with little room for error, and during extracation and stowage there was always a danger of damage to the fragile airframe. (Deutsches U-Boot Museum)

The Indian Ocean, and homeward bound

Since his exploits alongside *Komet* had resulted in greatly increased Allied naval activity as they searched for the German raiders, Weyher was ordered to head for the Indian Ocean, reaching his new area of operations without further engagements on 15 March 1941. The coming months were to be frustrating; however, Weyher made a number of rendezvous with refuelling and resupply ships, and finally received a long-awaited replacement Arado floatplane. Essential repairs were made to *Orion*'s by now worn-out engines, but the raider was desperately in need of a serious refit, and on 22 June 1941 her shaft bearings collapsed and she started taking on water. Having arranged a meeting with Capt Bernhard Rogge's auxiliary cruiser *Atlantis*, Weyher limped his way to the rendezvous, which took place on 1 July. After transferring sufficient fuel to *Orion* to ensure that she would be able to make it home, *Atlantis* headed off towards the Indian Ocean and Pacific while *Orion* sailed westwards, disguised at the Japanese freighter *Yuyo Maru*.

Finally, on 29 July 1941, as the raider headed northwards and after eight months without any victories, she intercepted the freighter *Chaucer*. Not one of the ten torpedoes fired at her by *Orion* detonated, and the Allied ship returned fire and started sending distress signals (though fortunately for Weyher, the position she radioed was out by more than 200 miles). *Orion* was forced to subdue the *Chaucer* by gunfire alone, eventually sinking her after 58 salvoes. All of the British crew were rescued.

Continuing to head northwards, *Orion*, now disguised as a Spanish freighter, reached the Bay of Biscay on 20 August; she was met by an escort of German destroyers, and led safely into Bordeaux. As the battered but triumphant raider entered port every ship in the harbour sounded its siren in tribute. *Orion* had been at sea for 510 days, had travelled more than 127,000 miles, and had sunk 77,000 tons of Allied shipping. Every member of her crew was awarded the Auxiliary Cruiser War Badge, and on 24 August, Capt Kurt Weyher formally learned that he had been awarded the Knight's Cross of the Iron Cross.

Orion was subsequently retired from active service and, renamed as *Hektor*, was used first as a repair ship and later as a training ship. In the closing months of the war she was activated once again as *Orion*, and employed in the evacuation of troops and refugees through the Baltic, being responsible for saving over 20,000 lives. She finally met her fate on 4 May 1945, when she had to be beached after suffering severe damage in an attack by Soviet aircraft. The wreck was scrapped in 1952.

ATLANTIS
HSK 2; Schiff 16; Raider C

Specification:			
Built	Bremer Vulkan, Bremen	Powerplant	2x MAN diesels
Launched	1937	Top speed	17.5 knots
Original name	*Goldenfels*	Endurance	60,000 n/miles
Length	155m	Armament	6x 15cm guns, 1x 7.5cm, 2x 3.7cm, 4x 2cm; 4x torpedo tubes; up to 92 mines; 2x Heinkel He114 floatplanes
Beam	18.6m		
Displacement	7,860 tons	Crew	347

Operational History

Destined to be the most famous of these commerce-raiders, the freighter *Goldenfels* underwent conversion into the auxiliary cruiser HSK 2 at Deschimag in Bremen during 1939, and on 19 December that year was formally commissioned into the Kriegsmarine under command of Kapitän zur See Bernhard Rogge. Her first few weeks in service were spent in crew training and operating as a Sperrbrecher – a vessel to lead and escort others into and out of port through cleared channels in the minefields.

HSK 1 *ORION*

The first merchantman to undergo conversion to an auxiliary cruiser began her working life with the Hamburg-Amerika Passenger Line (HAPAG). Here, she is shown in her first wartime disguise in April 1940 as the Dutch merchantman *Beemsterdijk* – her cover during the long voyage up the Norwegian coast on her way to Iceland and the Denmark Strait. In strict accordance with international law at the time, as a neutral ship she carries her national colours painted on the hull side, along with her name and port of registration – Rotterdam.

Note the position of her funnel, just aft of the bridge superstructure. *Orion*'s 15cm main armament was all mounted above decks, concealed within false deckhouses. Her torpedo tubes were also mounted on deck, and the guns and torpedo tubes were cleared for action by folding down the false deckhouses and the panels along the edge of the hull sides, allowing the gun turrets to traverse. Her Arado Ar196 floatplane was carried in the forward hold.

HSK 2 *ATLANTIS*

The most famous of the raiders, and the most successful of them to survive, began her life as the freighter *Goldenfels* of the Hansa shipping line. Here she is seen in spring 1940 in the Indian Ocean, in the guise of the Dutch merchantman *Abbekerk*. Note that in contrast to *Orion* she has her funnel to the rear of the midships structure. *Atlantis* also occasionally carried a false second funnel, but in her case in the forward position. Again unlike *Orion*, the bulk of *Atlantis'* main armament was mounted below deck level. The four 15cm guns – two to port and two to starboard – were all mounted forward of the bridge, concealed by panels consisting of parts of the vertical hull plates and the horizontal deck plates; these hinged upwards to allow the guns to swing out. Two further guns were carried astern on the centreline of the ship, one concealed within a false deckhouse; the aftermost gun was not concealed, but since many merchant ships carried a single defensive gun astern its presence would not betray the raider's true nature. Two single torpedo tubes were mounted below decks on either side, revealed by raising hinged plates in the hull. Her floatplane was stowed in the forward hold.

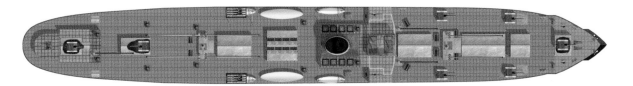

HSK 1 *ORION*

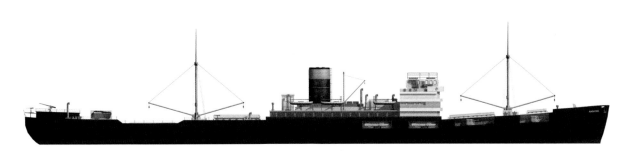

HSK 2 *ATLANTIS*

The most famous raider of them all, the *Atlantis* is seen here in her original identity as the *Goldenfels* in the livery of the Hansa line. Naturally, her conversion into an auxiliary cruiser would make few obvious outward alterations, since her effectiveness depended upon her retaining the appearance of a harmless merchantman. (Deutsches U-Boot Museum)

On 23 March 1940 her military livery was overpainted and her second funnel, added during conversion for military service, removed as she took on her first disguises – originally as the Norwegian *Knute Nielsen*, then as the Soviet auxiliary *Kim*. For the second of these impersonations Rogge even had one of the ship's Heinkel floatplanes painted with Soviet markings and left in full view on deck. Protected by poor weather, the new raider, christened *Atlantis* by her captain, headed north along the coast of Norway, intending to take the usual course around the top of the British Isles and through the Denmark Strait into the Atlantic. Her high speed and the cover of poor visibility in heavy seas allowed her to reach the Atlantic on 8 April, and two weeks later the raider had crossed the Equator into the South Atlantic.

His ship now disguised as the Japanese *Kasii Maru*, Rogge intercepted and sank the British freighter *Scientist* with a combination of torpedoes and gunfire; he was able to rescue nearly all of the British crew before heading south. On 10 May, Capt Rogge laid mines off Cape Agulhas before heading eastwards along the coast of South Africa and into the Indian Ocean.

Kapitän zur See Bernhard Rogge of HSK 2 *Atlantis*, the sole recipient of the Auxiliary Cruiser War Badge with Diamonds. Rogge went on to have a successful career in the West German Navy after the war. (Deutsches U-Boot Museum)

The Indian Ocean

On 21 May, Rogge changed his ship's disguise once again, this time to the Dutch *Abbekerk*. On June 10 he spotted a new target, and after a long chase caught up with the Norwegian *Tirranna*. The intended victim did not give up easily, and returned fire in a three-hour battle as she zig-zagged to avoid the raider's shells, before finally surrendering. The *Tirranna* was carrying valuable foodstuffs; a prize crew was placed on board to await refuelling for the return to Germany. Rogge now changed his disguise once again, to appear as the *Tarifa*. Weeks of inactivity dragged by until 11 July 1940, when a British ship was spotted. Rogge gave chase and ordered her to stop; her distress calls were silenced by a well-placed shot from one of *Atlantis*' guns into her radio shack. The *City of Baghdad* was swiftly captured and sunk, her crew taken being aboard the raider.

Two days later *Atlantis* intercepted a large cargo-liner; when Rogge fired warning shots she immediately signalled her intention to stop and requested medical assistance, without sending a distress call. Believing he had captured a suitable ship onto which to transfer his prisoners Rogge drew near, and was enraged when the stern gun on the ship, the *Kemmendine*, opened fire. The return fire from *Atlantis* set her ablaze, and far from unloading his prisoners Rogge was obliged to take on board even more before sinking her with torpedoes.

Rogge then rendezvoused with the *Tirranna* with the intention of transferring some fuel to her and sending her home loaded with the prisoners. At this stage an incident occurred that illustrates why Rogge earned the respect of his enemies. The commanding officer of the prize crew on *Tirranna* discovered that some of his men had rifled through the captured mailbags on board, and had stolen some items of value including the captain's binoculars. Despite his insistence that all stolen items be returned the binoculars remained missing. When this was reported to Rogge he offered to take no further action if the binoculars were returned. On learning the identity of the culprit, and that he had thrown the binoculars overboard for fear of being caught with them, he had the sailor court-martialled and sentenced to two years' imprisonment, discharged from the Navy in disgrace – and forced to pay compensation to the Norwegian captain.

While fuel and supplies were being transferred to *Tirranna* another ship appeared, approaching at some speed. *Atlantis* immediately raced towards her, and after a few warning shots were fired she surrendered. This was in fact the *Talleyrand*, a sister-ship of the *Tirranna* which had stumbled on the scene, assuming that *Tirranna* had broken down and was being helped by another merchantman. The fuel bunkers of the new prize were used to top up *Tirranna*, then the *Talleyrand* was used for target practice until she sank. *Tirranna* then set off for Germany under the prize crew; she made it all the way to the French coast, but tragically, while waiting for an escort into port, she was torpedoed and sunk by a British submarine, resulting in the loss of many of the lives that Rogge had saved.

Rogge's successes continued with the British *King City*, intercepted and sunk on 24 August off Madagascar. On 9 September she was followed to the bottom by the tanker *Athelking*, caught and sunk by gunfire, and just one day later the *Benarty* joined the growing list of the raider's victims. Her crew were taken off before she was sent to the bottom, and *Benarty* also yielded a number of Admiralty documents which enabled Capt Rogge's communications personnel to partially break the current British codes.

Rogge's next action came on 19 September, when the liner *Commissaire Ramel* obeyed the order to heave to and indicated that she would surrender. Rogge's hope of capturing a large and valuable prize was shattered when, despite having surrendered, the liner suddenly started to send out distress

Atlantis is shown here with an extra dummy funnel rigged immediately behind the bridge superstructure; this could be disassembled and removed very quickly when necessary. (Deutsches U-Boot Museum)

signals, obliging him to open fire to silence her. This caused heavy damage, and after picking up the survivors Rogge sent the stricken liner to the bottom. *Atlantis* was now carrying almost 300 prisoners in addition to her own crew.

After this action Rogge took *Atlantis* out of the shipping lanes, drifting slowly while his crew serviced the diesel engines. He recommenced operations on 1 October 1940, but it was to be three weeks before another target was found. On that day Rogge intercepted the Yugoslav *Durmitor*, which was technically neutral, but on finding she was headed for an Allied port Rogge claimed her as a prize and sent her on to Somaliland, at that time occupied by Germany's Italian allies.

Atlantis claimed her next victim on 8 November in the Bay of Bengal when she stopped and captured the tanker *Teddy* without having to fire a shot, after fooling the captain into believing that the raider was a British auxiliary cruiser. The valuable cargo of diesel and fuel oil was a godsend to the German crew, who despatched the *Teddy* to a rendezvous spot to meet her again later.

Two days later Rogge captured yet another tanker by using a similar ruse, this time the Norwegian *Ole Jacob*; unfortunately she was carrying high octane aviation fuel, useless for *Atlantis'* diesel motors, and she was sent to meet with *Teddy* and await further instructions from Rogge.

On 11 November an unidentified ship was spotted coming up on *Atlantis* from astern. Rogge slowed to allow her to catch up, then suddenly turned across her bows and ordered her to stop. Instead she maintained full speed and immediately started sending distress signals, so Rogge opened fire, destroying her bridge and wireless room. When the vessel eventually stopped the reason for her determined behaviour became clear: the *Automedon* was carrying aircraft, vehicles, military supplies and spare machine parts, as well as numerous documents with details of British defences in Singapore. The Germans were also pleased to find several hundred cases of whisky, several million cigarettes, and both fresh and frozen food. After they had salvaged as much of the cargo as possible the *Automedon* was sunk with demolition charges.

Rogge then rendezvoused with the *Ole Jacob*, transferring prisoners to her and sending her on to the port of Kobe in then-neutral Japan, where the cargo of aviation fuel was traded to the Japanese in exchange for diesel. On 8 December 1940, *Atlantis* met up with the auxiliary cruiser HSK 5 *Pinguin* and the two were then joined by the captured tanker *Storstad*; *Atlantis* was fully refuelled, and during the course of this meeting Capt Rogge received a signal informing him that he had been awarded the Knight's Cross.

Atlantis then sailed south for the Kerguelen Archipelago, where the crew were allowed to rest while much-needed repairs and maintenance work were carried out. Almost a full month later she set sail again for warmer waters, her next encounter being in the rich hunting-grounds between India and Madagascar. Bombed by the raider's floatplane, which also dragged its radio aerials away with towed grappling hooks, the *Mandasor* was devastated by a full broadside from *Atlantis*. On 31 January 1941, Capt Rogge intercepted and captured the British freighter *Speybank* without a shot being fired; and on 2 February the *Ketty Brovig* was also captured intact, with a valuable cargo of fuel oil and diesel. *Atlantis* then met up with the supply ship

The same view moments later, with the fake storage crate quickly cleared away to reveal a turret mounting a powerful 15cm gun. Note also how the collapsible ventilators have been folded down to lie on the deck. (Deutsches U-Boot Museum)

Here *Atlantis* is disguised as a Japanese freighter, the *Kasii Maru*, complete with a large hinomaru red sun flag on the hull side. In 1940–41 Japan was still neutral and many Japanese merchant ships plied the Pacific sea-lanes, making them good candidates for this sort of imposture. (Deutsches U-Boot Museum)

Tannenfels and, with *Speybank* and *Ketty Brovig*, rendezvoused with the heavy cruiser *Admiral Scheer*, each one of the small flotilla sharing out parts of their vital cargoes with the others.

The South Atlantic

After several fruitless weeks *Atlantis* rounded the Cape of Good Hope into the South Atlantic where, on 17 April 1941, she intercepted what Rogge believed was a British troopship. He opened fire; the vessel had indeed once been a troopship, but she was now the *Zam Zam*, under Egyptian ownership as a liner carrying civilian passengers (although the fact that she was also carrying war materials for the British made her a legitimate target). Unluckily for Rogge, she was also carrying many neutral Americans, some of whom were journalists equipped with cameras. The prisoners onboard *Atlantis* were subsequently transferred to the supply ship *Dresden* on 26 April, and transported to safety in France. Ultimately the information and photographs gathered by the American journalists would fall into British hands, and would eventually assist them in tracking down 'Raider C'.

Atlantis claimed her next victim on 13 May when she stopped and sank the British freighter *Rabaul* off the west coast of Africa. Five days later,

Looking up from sea level, this view shows both of the *Atlantis'* port side 15cm forward guns unmasked. Note the hinged hull panels, complete with deck railings, swung up to clear the guns; these panels were a close fit, and would not be noticeable from any distance. (Deutsches U-Boot Museum)

the British battleship HMS *Nelson* in consort with an aircraft carrier passed just astern of the raider without spotting her. On 24 May, the freighter *Trafalgar* with a cargo of coal was sent to the bottom. The *Tottenham*, carrying war materials including trucks and aircraft, was intercepted and sunk on 17 June, and on the 22nd the *Balzac*, carrying a cargo of foodstuffs, became Rogge's next victim.

By now, after 15 months at sea, both the ship and her crew were tired out. Rogge took *Atlantis* out of the shipping lanes for a week of rest, recuperation and essential maintenance, before meeting up with HSK 1 *Orion* to provide her with some fuel.

Two fatal rendezvous

Atlantis now headed south-west and rounded Cape Horn, heading into the Pacific. Here, on 10 September, Rogge intercepted and captured the freighter *Silvaplana*. On 21 September, *Atlantis* met up with the auxiliary cruiser *Komet* and the supply ship *Munsterland* at a pre-arranged rendezvous, where she was able to take on supplies and transfer her prisoners. The raider then gradually cruised eastwards, back around Cape Horn to re-enter the South Atlantic.

On 13 November 1941 *Atlantis* kept a rendezvous with U-68 in order to refuel the submarine, and on 22 November with U-126.

A view looking down into the gun deck of *Atlantis* with a 15cm gun turret trained out to port. Although the guns carried by the auxiliary cruisers were of obsolete models they were more than adequate for the task required of them. (Deutsches U-Boot Museum)

Refuelling was underway when the two German vessels were surprised by the sudden appearance of the cruiser HMS *Devonshire*. The U-boat commander, Kapitänleutnant Ernst-Ludwig Bauer, was stranded on board *Atlantis* when his submarine was forced to crash dive. The raider was no match for the 8-in. guns of the British cruiser, and an attempt to pass herself off as the Dutch freighter *Polyphemus* was frustrated by the fact that the British were able to identify her from photos taken by the American journalists who had been on the *Zam Zam*.

Atlantis was now taking a heavy pounding from the cruiser, which stood off out of range of the raider's lighter guns. Realizing that there was no hope, Capt Rogge ordered a smokescreen laid, and under its cover his crew set scuttling charges and abandoned ship. Seeing that the survivors of the *Atlantis* were being picked up by the various rafts and boats, and bearing in mind that there was a German submarine in the immediate area, HMS *Devonshire* departed.

U-126 then surfaced and, taking the motley collection of boats, rafts and floating debris in tow, radioed for assistance and began heading for the coast of South America. Two days later the supply ship *Python* appeared and took the survivors aboard. *Python* was under orders to meet and resupply a number of other U-boats on her way home; and during one of these rendezvous another British warship appeared – the cruiser HMS *Dorsetshire*, sister of the ship that had sunk the *Atlantis*. As the U-boats crash-dived *Python* turned tail but, straddled by shots from the warship, she too was scuttled. Once again the crew of *Atlantis* found themselves in the water, joined this time by the complement of the *Python*, and once again the known presence of U-boats obliged the British cruiser to retire.

A rescue mission was then launched by a number of U-boats, each of which crammed every spare inch of its hull with rescued German sailors. The last of these men finally reached France on 29 December 1941. A grateful Grossadmiral Raeder authorized leave and promotion to petty officer for every crewman, and a promotion of one rank for every officer. Rogge was decorated with the Oakleaves to his Knight's Cross, and Raeder presented him with a special version of the Auxiliary Cruiser War Badge in solid silver with a diamond-studded swastika.

Bernhard Rogge survived the war, and went on to serve in the West German Bundesmarine. He died in Hamburg on 29 June 1982.

WIDDER
HSK 3; Schiff 21; Raider D

Specification:			
Built	Howaldtswerke, Kiel	Powerplant	2x Blohm & Voss turbines
Launched	1929	Top speed	15 knots
Original name	*Neumark*	Endurance	34,000 n/miles
Length	152m	Armament	6x 15cm guns, 1x 7.5cm, 2x 3.7cm, 4x 2cm; 4x torpedo tubes; 2x Heinkel He114 floatplanes
Beam	18.2m		
Displacement	7,850 tons	Crew	363

B

HSK 3 *WIDDER*
Captain von Ruckteschell's first raiding command was a sister-ship to the *Orion*, and was completed with an almost identical layout (though she carried a much smaller load of sea mines, and different aircraft). Despite her captain's controversial tactics of attacking without warning, *Widder* was the less successful of the two in terms of Allied shipping sunk.

HSK 4 *THOR*
The former *Santa Cruz* of the OPDR line had a displacement of only 3,860 tons, and her size became something of a problem when the number of sailors taken prisoner from the vessels she had sunk outnumbered the German crew. All of *Thor's* main armament was mounted on deck, hidden from view by either false deckhouses or hinged plates on the hull side. Her single torpedo tubes were mounted on the main deck just under the boat deck.

AIRCRAFT
The purpose of carrying aircraft on the auxiliary cruisers was twofold. Most importantly, they could greatly extend her search radius, scouting relatively far afield to search for new targets below the horizon, and equally giving the raider early warning of the approach of an Allied warship. However, on some occasions the aircraft from the *Atlantis* and *Thor* (see Plate C) also took a direct part in interceptions, dropping small bombs or destroying a merchantman's radio antennae with grappling hooks towed on a cable.

Heinkel 114, as carried on *Atlantis*, *Widder* and *Pinguin*. This type was later superseded by the Arado Ar196, a fine aircraft that eventually became the standard shipboard floatplane on major warships.

Arado 231, carried only on *Stier*; this type proved not nearly robust enough for the repeated handling, extractions, take-offs, landings and recoveries on the open ocean.

B

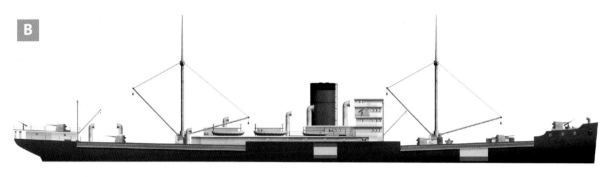

HSK 3 *WIDDER*

HSK 4 *THOR*

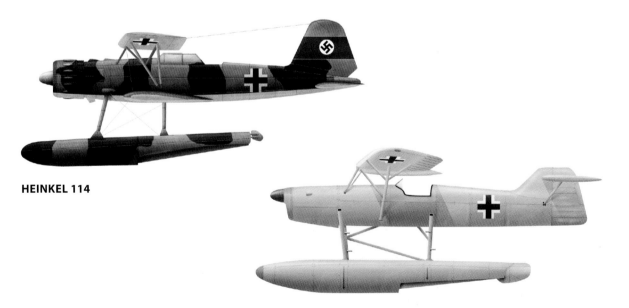

HEINKEL 114

ARADO 231

Operational History

A sister-ship to *Orion*, this vessel began life as the *Neumark*; converted into an auxiliary cruiser at the Blohm & Voss yard in Hamburg, she was commissioned into the Kriegsmarine on 30 November 1939 under the command of Korvettenkapitän Hellmuth von Ruckteschell. After completing her trails and crew training in the Baltic, the new raider, christened *Widder*, departed on 5 May 1940 for operations in the Atlantic. She followed the usual course up the Norwegian coast, around Great Britain and down through the Denmark Strait, but the journey was not without incident. *Widder* was fortunate to escape when she was intercepted by a British submarine, which exchanged gunfire with the raider, but the two separated without either scoring any hits. *Widder* eventually entered the Atlantic on 20 May 1940, and reached her initial area of operations six days later.

She found her first target on 13 June, when she surprised the tanker *British Petrol*, whose radio room was destroyed by shells from what appeared to be a neutral Swedish merchantman. Being in ballast with no useful cargo, the tanker was of no use to Capt von Ruckteschell, and after her crew were taken aboard she was despatched with a torpedo. On 26 June another tanker, the Norwegian *Krossfon*, was intercepted and persuaded to surrender without a shot fired; this one was sent back to France with a prize crew, and subsequently served in the Kriegsmarine as the *Spichern*.

Widder's next victory was to be controversial. On 7 July the raider intercepted the British freighter *Motomar*; once again the intended target accepted the raider's neutral guise until it was too late, and *Widder* opened fire, shooting away her antennae and radio room. The freighter indicated its intention to surrender, but on seeing some men running towards the 4-in. gun on the stern Capt von Ruckteschell ordered his light flak cannon to fire, killing or wounding several of them. A boarding party identified the ship as the *Davisian*; after her surviving crew were evacuated to the *Widder* she was sunk by a combination of demolition charges and torpedoes.

Six days later the British freighter *King John* became *Widder*'s next victim. Not wishing to load his ship with prisoners, von Ruckteschell took only the captain and chief engineer; the remainder of her crew – along with the prisoners already aboard *Widder* – were ordered into the lifeboats, given food, water, sails and compasses, and directed

to the Lesser Antilles, a journey which took them around seven days. This was another decision that would come back to haunt the raider's captain.

Widder then changed her disguise to appear as the Spanish *El Neptuno*, and on 4 August 1940 intercepted the Norwegian tanker *Beaulieu*. Using his normal tactic, Capt von Ruckteschell approached the unsuspecting tanker and opened fire without warning. The bulk of the crew abandoned ship, and made off in the lifeboats to avoid being taken prisoner. The raider's captain made no effort to search for them; a number of his officers were unhappy at this decision, and they prevailed upon him to show greater compassion for survivors in future. Four days later *Widder* sank the Dutch freighter *Oostplein* with a mixture of gunfire and torpedoes after the surviving crew had been picked up, and on 10 August the captain added the sailing ship *Killoran* to his tally; although she was a neutral Finnish vessel the cargo was British-owned, making her a legitimate target.

Thirteen days passed before another ship, this time the *Anglo Saxon*, would fall victim to von Ruckteschell's tactic of closing to almost point-blank range and opening fire without warning. On this occasion the barrage from *Widder* was so effective that virtually all of the freighter's boats were blown to pieces, leaving the survivors to struggle for their lives on a few rafts and one small jollyboat; a number of the crew were hit by gunfire from *Widder* while trying to abandon ship.

Korvettenkapitän Hellmuth von Ruckteschell, commander of the *Widder* and later the *Michel*, who died in prison in 1948 after being convicted of failing to show sufficient concern for the safety of the crews of the Allied merchantmen that he attacked without warning. (Deutsches U-Boot Museum)

On 2 September the tanker *Cymbeline* was intercepted in darkness, but despite being hit by devastating gunfire from *Widder* she continued to send distress signals, forcing Ruckteschell to continue firing until the tanker's radio was silenced. This time, despite the distress warning sent by the tanker, he lingered in the area for four hours looking for survivors. In fact the crew had taken to the boats and made off into the darkness.

Widder's next victim, on 8 September, was far less dramatic. Seeing a freighter approach his ship, Capt von Ruckteschell ordered her to stop, which she did without sending any radio signals. The crew of the *Antonios Chandris* were ordered to take what provisions they needed into the ship's boats and make for the coast of Africa, while the Germans set demolition charges.

The next few days were spent by *Widder*'s crew in trying to service the troublesome engines, before meeting up with the German supply ships *Eurofeld* and *Rekum*; many of the accumulated prisoners were transferred onto the latter.

Five days later, as she continued her patrol, *Widder*'s engines broke down completely, leaving her wallowing dead in the water. A full week of helpless drifting while the crew struggled to get her engines into some sort of working order left Capt von Ruckteschell concerned about his ability to continue his mission. With the engines running again, but overheating and vibrating heavily, he requested and received permission to curtail his cruise and head for home. *Widder* finally reached Brest on 31 October 1940 after 178 days at sea.

The reward awaiting Hellmuth von Ruckteschell was the Knight's Cross; every officer was awarded the Iron Cross 1st Class, and every crewman the 2nd Class. *Widder* eventually made her way back to Germany, where the worn-out vessel was decommissioned, eventually returning to service as a supply/repair ship.

* * *

The tactic employed by most raiders was to draw near to the victim, then send a signal ordering it to heave to and not to use the radio. Only if this instruction was disobeyed would the raider open fire – aiming at the freighter's bridge area to destroy her antennae and radio room. The method used by Capt von Ruckteschell, of opening fire without giving warning, and what was seen as his lack of concern for survivors, gained him a reputation for brutality. After the war he was arraigned on five counts of war crimes. In 1947 he was sentenced to 10 years' imprisonment, but although this sentence was later reduced he died of a heart attack in prison in June 1948.

THOR
HSK 4; Schiff 10; Raider E

Specification:			
Built	Deutsche Werft, Hamburg	Powerplant	2x AEG turbines
Launched	1938	Top speed	18 knots
Original name	*Santa Cruz*	Endurance	40,000 n/miles
Length	122m	Armament	6x 15cm guns, 1x 6cm, 2x 3.7cm, 4x 2cm; 4x torpedo tubes; 1x Arado Ar196 floatplane
Beam	16.7m		
Displacement	3,860 tons	Crew	349

Operational history
The former freighter *Santa Cruz* was converted into an auxiliary cruiser at the Deutsche Werft yard in Hamburg, and commissioned on 15 March 1940 under the command of Kapitän zur See Otto Kähler.

On 6 June 1940, *Thor* set off on her first war cruise, stopping off in Norway to don a disguise as a Russian freighter before breaking out into the Atlantic through the Denmark Strait on 16 June. Her first success came on 1 July when, now disguised as a Yugoslav merchantman, she intercepted the Dutch *Kertosono*, which surrendered without resistance and was sent safely back to Lorient as a prize. Six days later, having crossed the Equator into the South Atlantic, she intercepted the British *Delambre* after a two-hour chase; her crew were taken aboard before she was scuttled. Two days later the Belgian *Bruges* was also halted without giving the alarm, and sent to the bottom with demolition charges. *Thor*'s run of good luck continued on 14 July, when the freighter *Gracefield* also hove to when ordered; not one of the raider's four victims had made any attempt to send distress signals.

On 16 July, however, the British *Wendover* fled and immediately radioed distress signals when fired upon. She was soon persuaded to stop, and once her crew were aboard the raider she was sunk by a combination of torpedoes and gunfire. However, *Thor* – one of the smaller auxiliary cruisers, not much more than half the size of HSK 1, 2 & 3 – now had almost 200 prisoners on board to feed and care for. The strain on the stores was somewhat eased the next day when the Dutch freighter *Tela* also surrendered after a single warning shot; she carried a cargo of foodstuffs which replenished the raider's supplies, though it did nothing to ease the cramped conditions below decks.

After a quiet couple of weeks, on 28 July the lookouts spotted what turned out to be the British 22,000-ton armed merchant cruiser HMS *Alcantara*. Captain Kähler had no wish for such a confrontation; *Thor* turned and sped off, but the British warship followed, demanding that she identify herself. Knowing that the British ship had the greater turn of speed, Kähler turned across her bows and, with the sun behind him to dazzle her gun crews, opened fire and scored several hits. The battle raged for over four hours, and despite taking a couple of hits herself *Thor* definitely had the better of her much larger opponent. Not wishing to risk his mission by taking more damage, Kähler ordered a smokescreen and withdrew, leaving the *Alcantara* to limp off towards neutral Brazil.

It was to be many weeks before *Thor* found her next victims; on 26 September the Norwegian *Kosmos III* was sunk by gunfire, and on 8 October the British freighter *Natia* joined her. Their survivors brought the number of prisoners aboard the raider to more than 360, greater than the number of her own crew. The next few weeks proved fruitless, however, and on 9 November *Thor* met with the German blockade-runner *Rio Grande*, which both resupplied the raider and took on board all but a handful of her prisoners for transportation back to Germany.

The raider's next victory came on 5 December 1940, when Kähler had the misfortune to run into yet another large armed merchant cruiser,

The original paybook of Dr Jürgen Harms, the ship's doctor of the *Thor*. In the identity photograph the Auxiliary Cruiser War Badge is visible on his tunic below his Iron Cross 1st Class. Dr Harms was mentioned in reports for the care given to prisoners held on board the raider. (Author's collection)

HMS *Carnarvon Castle*. Without the speed to outrun the larger ship, Kähler turned away from it to provide a smaller target whilst engaging the British vessel with his stern armament. His crews scored so many significant hits that *Carnarvon Castle* gave up the fight and departed. Twice now the diminutive *Thor* had fought off much larger enemy ships, and on 22 December 1940, Capt Otto Kähler was awarded the Knight's Cross for his achievements. On Christmas Day, *Thor* rendezvoused with the pocket battleship *Admiral Scheer*, and a refrigerated freighter which the *Admiral Scheer* had captured was able to provide the raider with large quantities of food for the festive season and well beyond.

The cruel sea

The next three months saw a number of resupply meetings with other German vessels but nothing in the way of targets. This dry season ended on 25 March 1941, when the British passenger ship *Britannia* was intercepted, with many naval and air force personnel amongst her passengers. Once the *Britannia* had been forced to stop and her passengers had taken to the lifeboats the ship was sunk by gunfire. As *Thor* was preparing to take the survivors on board a message was heard from another ship that was answering the *Britannia*'s distress signals, advising that it was approaching with all speed. Not wishing to wait around in case this was a warship, Kähler withdrew; tragically, the other ship never arrived, and around 200 of the British passengers and crew who had survived the sinking later lost their lives. Later that same day, Kähler stopped and sank with demolition charges the Swedish *Trolleholm*, under contract to the British.

On 4 April 1941, as *Thor* approached what Kähler believed to be a neutral passenger liner and fired a warning shot to persuade her to stop, the other vessel returned fire. Incredibly, Kähler had encountered yet another armed merchant cruiser, HMS *Voltaire*. This time, however, there was to be no breaking off the action; within a short time *Thor*'s superior gunnery had reduced the much larger ship to a blazing wreck, and white flags of surrender were soon run up. With the *Voltaire*'s lifeboats smashed during the action, Kähler launched his own boats to rescue almost 200 survivors.

Thor then headed north on the homeward leg of her highly successful cruise, and on 16 April intercepted the Swedish freighter *Sir Ernest Cassell* carrying a load of ore for the British. This ship would become *Thor*'s last victim; on 30 April 1941 the raider berthed in Hamburg, having sunk 12 Allied and neutral ships totalling 96,540 tons in the course of well over 57,000 miles, during almost a year at sea.

The second cruise

After a complete overhaul, *Thor* departed on her second cruise on 19 November 1941; her new commander was Kapitän zur See Günther Gumprich.

Disaster struck almost immediately when, in thick fog, *Thor* rammed a Swedish merchant ship, sinking her and suffering enough damage to force her to return for repairs. Eventually, after many delays, the raider reached the Atlantic by hugging the Dutch and French coasts through the English Channel rather than taking the northern route and the Denmark Strait. *Thor* crossed the Equator into the South Atlantic on 4 February 1942, and her first area of operations was to be in Antarctic waters; the hunt for Allied whalers was unsuccessful, however, and Capt Gumprich headed north again.

On 23 March he intercepted the Greek freighter *Pagasitikos*, which surrendered without resistance and was sunk by torpedo. After refuelling from the supply ship *Regensburg* the following day, Gumprich headed north for a rendezvous with Capt von Ruckteschell's new command, the auxiliary cruiser HSK 9 *Michel*, near St Helena in the South Atlantic. En route, on 30 March *Thor* intercepted the British freighter *Wellpark* and sank her with demolition charges. Just two days later the freighter *Willesden* had her radio aerials ripped away by grappling hooks trailed by *Thor*'s Arado floatplane to prevent her sending out distress signals, before being halted by the raider and sunk with torpedoes. The same tactics were used successfully on 3 April against the freighter *Aust*. One week later *Thor* carried out a night attack on the freighter *Kirkpool*; the British merchantman was so badly battered that all her boats were destroyed, so *Thor* had to remain on the scene for three hours picking up the survivors in her own boats.

Heading east into the Indian Ocean, on 10 May 1942 *Thor* seized the liner *Nankin* after a long chase and put a prize crew on board. Her next interception would leave worse memories: a warning shot fired at what Gumprich took to be a freighter struck what turned out to be the Dutch tanker *Olivia* and ignited her cargo, and 33 of her crew of 46 perished horribly. The next victim was another tanker, but this time a warning shot and the destruction of her antennae by the floatplane sufficed to persuade the *Herborg* to surrender; she was sent to Japan under a prize crew, and arrived safely. On 4 July the Norwegian tanker *Madrono* was taken in almost identical circumstances.

Thor's next victim showed fight; when ordered to stop the British freighter *Indus* returned fire and immediately started to send distress signals. The crew only abandoned ship when her radio room had been smashed and the vessel was fully ablaze.

With supplies and fuel now running low, *Thor* headed for Yokohama in Japan where a refit had been arranged. The raider docked there on 10 October, and was ready for sea

Kapitän zur See Otto Kähler, commander of the *Thor* during her first and highly successful war cruise. Kähler was decorated with the Knight's Cross on 22 December 1940 in recognition of his achievements. (Deutsches U-Boot Museum)

again seven weeks later. She was being re-provisioned while moored alongside the tanker *Uckermark*, which was having her fuel tanks cleaned out. A spark ignited the fume-filled tanks and blew the tanker apart; the resulting inferno destroyed not only the *Uckermark*, but also the *Thor* and a number of other vessels. Thirteen of the *Thor*'s crew were killed, but Gumprich and the majority of his men survived the disaster.

PINGUIN
HSK 5; Schiff 33; Raider F

Specification:			
Built	AG Weser, Bremen	Powerplant	1x MAN 6-cylinder diesel
Launched	1936	Top speed	17 knots
Original name	*Kandelfels*	Endurance	60,000 n/miles
Length	155m	Armament	6x 15cm guns, 1x 7.5, 2x 3.7cm, 4x 2cm; 2x torpedo tubes; up to 300 mines; 2x Heinkel He114 floatplanes, later 1x Arado Ar196
Beam	18.7m		
Displacement	7,760 tons	Crew	420

Operational history

The freighter *Kandelfels* was converted into an auxiliary cruiser at the Bremer Deschimag Werft in Bremen through late 1939/early 1940, and was commissioned into the Kriegsmarine on 6 February 1940 under the command of Kapitän zur See Ernst-Felix Krüder. After completing her trials and training exercises, *Pinguin* departed for the Atlantic on 15 June 1940, via the North Sea and Denmark Strait. Disguised as a Soviet merchantman she broke out into the North Atlantic on 1 July, changing her disguise to that of the Greek freighter *Kassos*.

On 20 July she carried out a resupply exercise with the submarine U-A off the Cape Verde Islands before sailing south and, on 31 July, attacking and sinking the British freighter *Domingo de Larrinaga* by torpedo.

Pinguin rounded Cape Horn into the Pacific on 20 August, and six days later captured the Norwegian tanker *Filefjell* intact. On the following day another tanker, the *British Commander*, was intercepted, but this time the target fled while transmitting distress signals. *Pinguin* pursued, and subdued her with gunfire and torpedoes. No sooner had *Pinguin* picked up the survivors and left the scene than she ran into yet another freighter, the

HSK 4 *THOR* CAPTURES THE TANKER *HERBORG*, 19 JUNE 1942

The Norwegian tanker *Herborg* was in the Indian Ocean en route from Abadan to Fremantle when she was intercepted by the auxiliary cruiser *Thor* on 19 June 1942. The tanker was armed with a single 3-in. gun on her stern manned by a Chinese crew, primarily as a defence against surfaced submarines. Captain Gumprich sent his Ar196 floatplane into the attack, using a grappling hook to tear away the tanker's radio aerials and dropping two small bombs. When the *Thor* then fired a warning shot from one of her 15cm guns and ran up her battle ensign, the tanker's captain wisely decided not to offer any resistance. Having drawn closer to her victim, *Thor* is seen here sending over a Prizenkommando or prize crew to take control of the Allied vessel and her valuable 11,000-ton cargo of oil. The *Herborg* was renamed *Hohenfriedberg* by the Germans and sent on to Japan, where she and her cargo arrived safely. The tanker's officers were held on *Thor*, while the bulk of her crew were dispersed onto a number of other vessels and shipped back to Europe. The former *Herborg* was later sent to France as a blockade-runner, but was intercepted en route and sunk by the British.

brand-new Norwegian *Morviken*, which surrendered and was scuttled after her crew had been taken aboard the raider. Moving to an area a safe distance from the shipping lanes, Krüder had *Filefjell's* fuel oil transferred to *Pinguin*, then sank the tanker.

On 12 September the freighter *Benavon* was intercepted and ordered to stop; she failed to do so, and when a warning shot was fired she returned fire, scoring a hit on *Pinguin*. The freighter was no match for the raider, however, and was soon silenced; her survivors were taken aboard and the blazing hulk of the *Benavon* was left to burn itself out.

Pinguin's next encounter, on 16 September, was trouble-free; the Norwegian freighter *Nordvard* stopped when ordered and did not use her radio. Captain Krüder placed a prize crew aboard and started her on the long voyage back to France. *Pinguin*'s next victim was also Norwegian and also docile – the tanker *Storstad*, intercepted and captured without resistance on 7 October. A prize crew was put on board with the intention of using her as a minelayer for *Pinguin*, and the two ships then proceeded to lay mines in Australian waters; these sank five ships and damaged a sixth.

Antarctic waters

Pinguin then headed south to attack Allied whalers off Antarctica, and on 17 November intercepted, captured and scuttled the British freighter *Nowshera*. On 20 November, after a prolonged chase involving both *Pinguin* and her floatplane, the British freighter *Maimoa* was forced to stop and was scuttled in her turn. The following day the refrigerated transport ship *Port Brisbane* joined the raider's growing list of victims, forced to stop after being pounded by *Pinguin*'s main armament before being sunk with scuttling charges and torpedoes. Just two days later the refrigerated freighter *Port Wellington* was captured and sunk with scuttling charges. On 24 December 1940, Capt Krüder learned that he had been awarded the Knight's Cross.

Continuing to cruise the freezing southern ocean in search of the whaling fleet operating around South Georgia, on the early morning of 14 January 1941 *Pinguin* emerged out of the darkness to surprise two large whaling factory ships, *Ole Wegger* and *Solglimt*. Both swiftly surrendered, as did four small whalers. Later that same day *Pinguin* intercepted and captured another factory ship, the *Pelagos*, along with seven of her associated whale-catchers. After this tremendous success *Pinguin* would not meet her next victim until 25 April 1941, when she sank the British freighter *Empire Light*, and two days later another, the *Clan Buchanan*.

HSK 5 *Pinguin*, the most successful of all the raiders in terms of shipping sunk – 32 vessels totalling more than 154,000 tons – though not in the final outcome of her cruise: she was sunk with nearly all hands by the Royal Navy cruiser HMS *Cornwall*. (Courtesy M. Westley)

Most of the raiders counted sea mines as an essential part of their armament; *Pinguin* could carry up to 300, and in October 1940 those she laid in Australian waters sank several ships. The mines were stored below decks on small wheeled trolleys, which allowed them to be rolled along special rails and dropped through an opening in the ship's stern. (Deutsches U-Boot Museum)

On 7 May, by now heading towards the Persian Gulf, *Pinguin* gave chase to a small tanker – Capt Krüder was anxious to top up his fuel tanks. The *British Emperor* refused to submit and transmitted distress signals, forcing *Pinguin* to open fire. The tanker was soon ablaze, denying Krüder its cargo, and he finished her off with a torpedo. However, the tanker's warning signals had been picked up by the British cruiser HMS *Cornwall*, and on 8 May the raider was spotted by the cruiser's seaplane. The British were not completely taken in by *Pinguin*'s disguise and decided to investigate her more closely.

Pinguin maintained the pretence of being Norwegian until the very last moment, and only when *Cornwall* had fired a warning shot did she clear her guns and return fire. The uneven contest could not last for long, and the combined firepower of the cruiser's eight 8-in. guns caused devastating damage; one shell then penetrated the *Pinguin*'s magazines and detonated her stored mines, blowing the raider to pieces. Between her German crew and her unfortunate prisoners, *Pinguin* was carrying nearly 640 men; of these only 61 crew and 24 prisoners survived.

Pinguin had sailed more than 59,000 miles and was responsible for the sinking or capture of 32 ships totalling over 154,000 tons.

STIER
HSK 6; Schiff 23; Raider I

Specification:			
Built	Germaniawerft, Kiel	Powerplant	1x MAN 7-cylinder diesel
Launched	1936	Top speed	14.5 knots
Original name	*Cairo*	Endurance	50,000 n/miles
Length	134m	Armament	6x 15cm guns, 2x 3.7cm, 4x 2cm; 2x torpedo tubes; up to 230 mines; 2x Arado Ar231 floatlanes, 1x Schnellboot
Beam	17.3m		
Displacement	4,778 tons	Crew	325

One of the larger raiders, HSK 6 *Stier* shows the effects on her paintwork of a long cruise; nothing could be less like the neatly maintained appearance of a warship. *Stier* was the least successful of the auxiliary cruisers which got out into the open ocean, sinking only four Allied ships in the course of nearly six months at sea before her fatal encounter with the heroic captain and crew of the American freighter *Stephen Hopkins* on 27 Sepember 1942. (Deutsches U-Boot Museum)

Operational history

The freighter *Cairo* was converted at the Wilton-Fijenoord Werft in Schiedam and the Oder Werke in Stettin, and was commissioned into the Kriegsmarine under the command of Fregattenkapitän Horst Gerlach on 11 November 1941.

Unlike most of her fellow raiders *Stier*'s break-out into the Atlantic was not to be via the northern route but through the English Channel. The raider made it unscathed through these dangerous waters (though her escorts took something of a battering), and reached the open Atlantic on 20 May 1942.

Stier's first victim was encountered on 4 June, when the freighter *Gemstone* was intercepted in the South Atlantic, surrendered, and was sunk with torpedoes.

Two days later *Stier* fought a brief but fierce battle with the tanker *Stanvac Calcutta*; return fire hit one of *Stier*'s gun positions, killing the crew. The unequal battle could only have one outcome, however, and the battered tanker sank after being abandoned by its crew.

On 9 August *Stier* encountered the freighter *Dalhousie*, which surrendered after a brief chase and was sunk by torpedo.

 D

HSK 5 *PINGUIN*

The most successful of the commerce raiders in terms of shipping sunk began life as the *Kandelfels* with the Hansa line. She is seen here in her disguise as the neutral Greek freighter *Kassos* in July 1940; the Greek colours of a white cross on blue are emblazoned in three places along her hull side, and the name KASSOS GREECE is painted in large white letters amidships.

Like *Atlantis*, to which she was a sister-ship, *Pinguin* carried most of her main armament below deck level, though more evenly distributed. *Pinguin* only carried two single torpedo tubes, one mounted each side just aft of the main bridge superstructure and revealed by lifting hull panels. Again, her spotter floatplane was carried in the forward hold.

HSK 6 *STIER*

Formerly the *Cairo* of the Atlas-Levant line in Bremen, *Stier* was one of the larger raiders. Her guns were concealed within false deckhouses and no special folding hull plates were used. Interestingly, *Stier*'s two torpedo tubes, one on either side, were below the waterline. *Stier* met a unique fate when she was sunk by another armed merchant vessel, the US 'Liberty ship' *Stephen Hopkins*.

HSK 7 *KOMET*

The smallest of the raiders, the former freighter *Ems* was bought in from the Norddeutsche Lloyd line. Her four forward guns, two per side, were concealed behind folding plates; that on the after deck was concealed within a hold, and that at the stern was hidden from view by the lifeboats mounted either side. She carried her aircraft in the forward hold. The small LS-boat she carried was intended for use in minelaying rather than torpedo attacks.

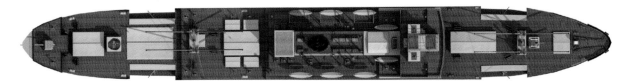

HSK 5 *PINGUIN*

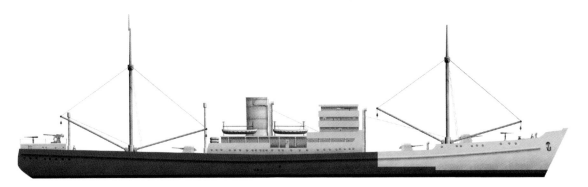

HSK 6 *STIER*

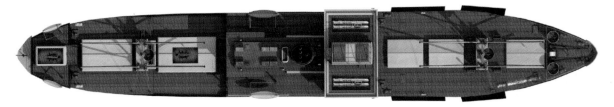

HSK 7 *KOMET*

On 27 September 1942, while sailing in company with the supply ship *Tannenfels*, the *Stier* encountered the US 'Liberty ship' *Stephen Hopkins*. When the raider fired a warning shot across her bows the American ship returned fire, and managed to achieve hits that put the *Stier*'s rudder and engines out of action. Both *Stier* and *Stephen Hopkins* continued to pour fire into one another, and although *Stier*'s superior firepower eventually reduced the freighter to a blazing hulk, the damage she herself sustained would prove fatal. With fires raging out of control below decks and his ship holed below the waterline, Capt Gerlach ordered his crew to abandon ship. The German crew and the few prisoners still on board were picked up by *Tannenfels* before the fires on *Stier* reached her load of torpedoes and blew her apart. This heroic action was the only occasion when an Allied freighter managed to destroy a German commerce raider, albeit at the cost of her own loss.

The commander of the *Stier*, Kapitän zur See Horst Gerlach. Subsequent to his service on the *Stier*, Gerlach was given command of the *Hansa*, and many of his former crew volunteered to serve with him again. In the event *Hansa* never saw active service, and Gerlach went on to serve in a number of shore-based commands. (Deutsches U-Boot Museum)

KOMET
HSK 7; Schiff 45; Raider B

Specification:			
Built	Deschimag, Bremen	Powerplant	2x MAN 6-cylinder diesels
Launched	1937	Top speed	16 knots
Original name	*Ems*	Endurance	35,000 n/miles
Length	115m	Armament	6x 15cm guns, 1x 6cm, 2x 3.7cm, 4x 2cm; 6x torpedo tubes; up to 30 mines; 2x Arado Ar196 floatplanes, 1x Schnellboot
Beam	15.3m		
Displacement	3,280 tons	Crew	274

Operational History

The freighter *Ems* was converted at the Howaldtswerke yard in Hamburg, and commissioned into the Kriegsmarine under the command of Kapitän zur See Robert Eyssen on 2 June 1940.

Unlike the other raiders, *Komet* reached her area of operations via the Arctic, aided by Soviet icebreakers – the Nazi-Soviet non-aggression pact was still in force. She sailed via the Barents Sea, on through the Bering Strait and eventually, on 10 September 1940, into the North Pacific. Eyssen's orders were to patrol the waters off the Australian coast and the Indian Ocean, and also to attack the Antarctic whaling fleets.

On 18 October 1940 he made a rendezvous with Capt Weyher's *Orion* at Lamottek Atoll in the Carolines, and the two raiders proceeded in company. It was to be 25 November before *Komet* achieved her first victory, when Eyssen intercepted the coaster *Holmwood*; she hove to when ordered, and Eyssen took the crew and passengers aboard *Komet* before scuttling her. Just two days later *Komet*'s lookouts spotted a large armed liner, the *Rangitane*; her captain refused Eyssen's orders to stop and began sending distress signals. *Komet* and *Orion* both opened fire, and with her radio wrecked the liner finally surrendered. Her crew and passengers were taken aboard and the liner's sea-cocks were opened, her end being hastened by a torpedo from *Komet*.

On 6 December 1940 the British freighter *Triona* – which had escaped from *Orion* in August – was halted and captured after a pursuit lasting several hours. The freighter was left with *Orion*, as *Komet* departed for an attack on the harbour of Nauru Island, west of the Gilberts group. En route Capt Eyssen encountered the freighter *Vinni*, which was swiftly captured

Komet's commander, Robert Eyssen, enjoyed a particularly successful career, reaching the rank of Konteradmiral while still in command of the raider. He subsequently served at Naval High Command. (Deutsches U-Boot Museum)

The crew are mustered on *Stier*'s deck as those killed in action are buried at sea with full naval honours; this photo was presumably taken following the engagement on 6 June 1942 with the armed tanker *Stanvac Calcutta*. Captain Gerlach can be seen in the centre of the shot, saluting as the dead sailor is committed to the deep. (Deutsches U-Boot Museum)

and scuttled. Meeting up with *Orion* again on 8 December, *Komet* made her approach to Nauru around the north of the island under the cover of darkness. Here she encountered the freighter *Komata*, which ignored Eyssen's orders to stop and began sending radio signals. *Komet* opened fire, destroying the freighter's radio room, whereupon the *Komata* surrendered and was sunk with scuttling charges. After putting most of his prisoners ashore on the island of Emirau, Eyssen returned to Nauru once again, where – after guaranteeing the safety of the harbour personnel if they remained in their living quarters – he shelled the port facilities, destroying wharves, cranes, and more than 13,000 tons of fuel.

Captain Eyssen now headed for the Indian Ocean, and on 1 January 1941 he received word that he had been promoted to Konteradmiral. There followed many fruitless months of wandering the great oceans, however, and Eyssen was ordered to return to Germany for a refit by October. He was gradually making his way northwards again in the eastern Pacific when, on 14 August 1941, he intercepted and sank the freighter *Australind* near the Galapagos Islands. On 17 August the Dutch freighter *Kota Nopan* was captured; her cargo of iron ore, tin, manganese and rubber was considered too important for her to be sunk, so permission was sought and received for the freighter to be refuelled and sent back to Germany with a prize crew aboard. Two days later another merchantman, the *Devon*, was captured and sunk by gunfire after her crew had been evacuated.

The smallest of all the auxiliary cruisers was the widely travelled HSK 7 *Komet* (3,280 tons). One of her Arado floatplanes can be seen sitting atop her forward hold. Most of the raiders encountered problems with their aircraft, none of which were really robust enough for the ocean-going mission. (Deutsches U-Boot Museum)

E HSK 8 *KORMORAN*

The sectional view shows the largest and most powerful of the auxiliary cruisers. The bulk of the conversion work involved adding weaponry; as a former merchant ship she already had large storage areas and holds that could be used with little alteration. Working aft from the bow: The upper three decks were given over to accommodation, both for the crew and for any prisoners, and for storage, while the lower levels accommodated fuel bunkers and an ammunition magazine. Just astern of the magazine sat more fuel bunkers, the ship's torpedo stores, and the electric motors.

Kormoran's four large diesel engines were mounted amidships, under the main provision stores, with further fuel bunkers and storerooms ahead and astern of the engine room.

Astern of the main stores was the mine storage area. The sea mines were fixed to small, weighted wheeled trolleys that also acted as the anchor for the mine. These wheeled trolleys ran on small rails right back to the stern of the ship, where they could be dropped through concealed openings. Astern of the mine stores on the ship's centreline were two large holds; the forward of these was used for stowing the ship's two Arado Ar196 floatplanes, and the aft hold for storing the ship's small motor torpedo boat.

Virtually all of *Kormoran*'s armament was well concealed, the only exception being a number of small 2cm anti-aircraft guns – if these were spotted they would not give rise to any real suspicion as to *Kormoran*'s true nature.

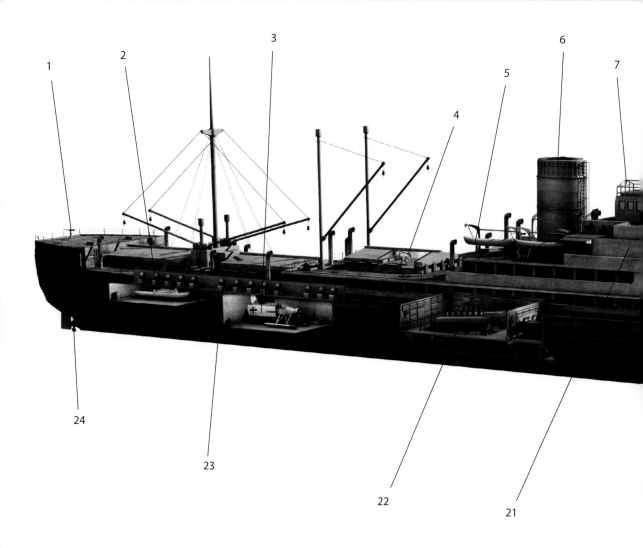

KEY

1   2cm anti-aircraft gun
2   Light torpedo boat LS-3
3   Arado Ar196 floatplane
4   Concealed 15cm gun in hold
5   Ship's boats
6   Funnel
7   Bridge
8   Derricks
9   Concealed 15cm gun within hold
10 Forward cargo hold
11 Concealed 15cm gun behind hull panels (one each side)
12 2cm anti-aircraft gun
13 Prisoner washroom

14 Prisoner accommodation
15 Stores
16 Accommodation for JNCOs and men
17 Mess for JNCOs and men
18 Magazine
19 Electric motor room
20 Triple 53cm torpedo tubes (one set each side)
21 Concealed 3.7cm gun behind superstructure panels (one each side)
22 Main 9 cylinder diesel engines
23 Sea mines on wheeled trolleys (rails running each side of hold)
24 Concealed 15cm guns behind stern panels (one each side)

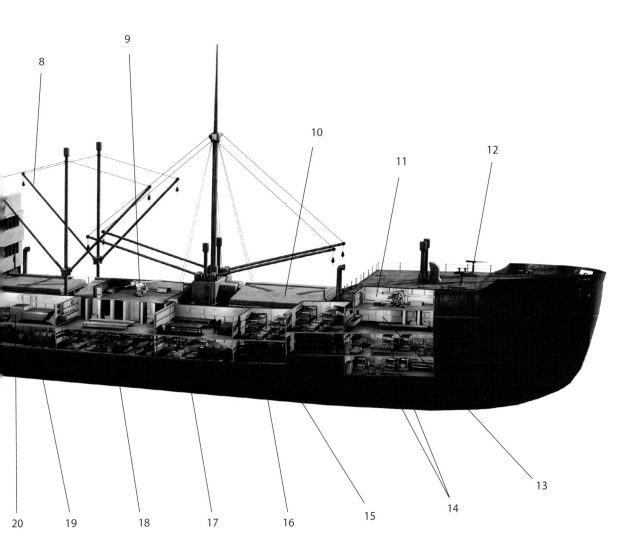

Komet is seen here during a meeting in the Pacific with a German supply vessel, the Anneliese Essberger. The raider is disguised as a neutral Japanese freighter again, note the 'meatball' flag visible on her hull side. Despite her small size she carried two floatplanes and a small motor torpedo boat. (Deutsches U-Boot Museum)

On her way home on 21 September, *Komet* rendezvoused with the supply ship *Munsterland* and Capt Rogge's raider *Atlantis* for an exchange of prisoners and provisions, and on 26 November 1941 she reached the Atlantic coast of France. Sailing on through the English Channel, she survived several attacks before anchoring safely in Hamburg on 30 November 1941 after 511 days at sea.

After a refit, it was intended that *Komet* should undertake a second cruise. Setting sail on 7 October 1942, she made for Boulogne; she survived attacks by Royal Navy MTBs, but a number of her escorts were lost to mines and she was obliged to take shelter in Dunkirk. On 12 October 1942, with an escort of torpedo boats, she attempted to break out down the Channel, but was intercepted by a force of British destroyers and MTBs. In the confused action that followed *Komet* was hit by two torpedoes and exploded soon afterwards, taking her entire crew down with her.

KORMORAN
HSK 8; Schiff 41; Raider G

Specification:			
Built	Germaniawerft, Kiel	Powerplant	4x Krupp-Germaniawerft 9-cylinder diesels
Launched	1938	Top speed	19 knots
Original name	*Steiermark*	Endurance	84,500 n/miles
Length	164m	Armament	6x 15cm guns, 1x 7.5cm, 2x 3.7cm, 5x 2cm; 6x torpedo tubes; up to 360 mines; 2x Arado Ar196 floatplanes, 1x Schnellboot
Beam	20.2m		
Displacement	8,730 tons	Crew	400

Operational History
The freighter *Steiermark* was converted into the largest and most powerful of the auxiliary cruisers at the Deutsche Werft in Hamburg, and commissioned into the Kriegsmarine on 9 October 1940 under the command of Korvettenkapitän Theodor Detmers. She set off on her war cruise on 3 December 1940, following the conventional course around the north of the British Isles and down through the Denmark Strait, reaching the Atlantic on 13 December under the cover of bad weather.

Her first victim was the Greek freighter *Antonis*, taken without resistance or radio traffic on 6 January 1941 and destroyed with demolition charges. On 18 January the tanker *British Union* was intercepted. When *Kormoran* fired a warning shot the tanker returned fire, but was soon halted by the raider's superior firepower; the crew abandoned the blazing ship, which was finished off with demolition charges. On 29 January *Kormoran* had a particularly successful day. She captured the refrigerated transport ship *Afric Star* in the early afternoon, sinking her with a mixture of demolition charges and torpedoes; and just three hours later Capt Detmers intercepted the British freighter *Eurylochus*, with a cargo of twin-engine bomber aircraft, and sank her with torpedoes.

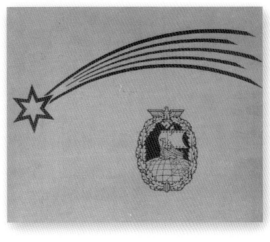

A special commemorative photo album was produced for crew members of the *Komet*, its cover bearing both the Auxiliary Cruiser War Badge and that raider's shooting star emblem. (Author's collection)

A few days later *Kormoran* rendezvoused with a supply ship to refuel and hand over her prisoners, before continuing to head south with the intention of rounding the Cape of Good Hope to operate in the Indian Ocean. On 25 February 1941 she met with Capt Krüder's raider *Pinguin*, and took on board some spares needed to repair *Kormoran*'s troublesome engines. On 22 March the tanker *Agnita* was intercepted and sunk with torpedoes, and just three days later the Canadian freighter *Canadolite* was captured and a prize crew put on board, along with *Kormoran*'s prisoners; the prize eventually reached France safely. On 9 April the British freighter *Craftsman* was chased down after she tried to run, and was sunk with demolition charges and torpedoes.

HSK 8 *Kormoran* was the largest and most powerful of the auxiliary cruisers, a fact attested to by her sinking of the cruiser HMAS *Sydney* during her last battle. (Deutsches U-Boot Museum)

Three days later a radio signal informed Detmers that he had been promoted to Fregattenkapitän, and on that same day his next victim appeared. However, the Greek freighter *Nicolaos DL* was carrying a cargo of timber, which kept her afloat even after her hull had been ripped open with

Kapitän zur See Theodor Detmers, commander of the *Kormoran*. Along with his surviving crew Detmers spent the rest of the war in an Australian POW camp, and received his Knight's Cross, awarded in December 1941, via the Red Cross while he was in captivity. (Deutsches U-Boot Museum)

demolition charges and torpedoes. Captain Detmers eventually gave up and left her to sink in her own time, as he departed for a rendezvous with Capt Rogge's *Atlantis*.

It was to take more than two months' cruising in the Indian Ocean before Detmers would find another target. On the morning of 26 June 1941 the Yugoslav freighter *Velebit* was battered by gunfire and left to drift onto a reef off the Andaman Islands. At around noon the same day *Kormoran* spotted and pursued the Australian freighter *Mareeba*, catching her after slowing her down with gunfire, and sinking her with demolition charges. This was to be the last victory for some time; fully three months would pass before Detmers captured and sank the Greek freighter *Embiricos* on 23 September. A further resupply rendezvous was carried out successfully before *Kormoran* headed for the waters off the Australian coast.

HMAS *Sydney*

There, on 19 November 1941, the raider met her match when she encountered the Australian cruiser HMAS *Sydney*. Detmers' attempt to pass his ship off as the Dutch merchantman *Straat Malakka* gained valuable time while the warship approached ever closer to *Kormoran*'s concealed guns – essential if the German raider was to have any chance of off-setting the advantage of the *Sydney*'s far longer-ranged firepower. A distress signal sent from *Kormoran* and acknowledged from an Australian coastal radio station served to confuse *Sydney* even further. Eventually, with the range down to a mere thousand yards, *Kormoran* ran up her battle flag, cleared her guns, and opened fire on the cruiser with both her main armament and with torpedoes.

Detmers' gun crews achieved devastating hits on the *Sydney*'s bridge and put her forward turrets out of action. The Australian ship's aft turrets scored a number of hits on *Kormoran* before they too were silenced, and both ships were on fire and badly damaged as they drifted apart. Night was falling, and after a huge explosion was heard the glow of the burning *Sydney* was seen no more. It is probable that the flames reached her magazines; there were no survivors.

Kormoran too had been fatally damaged, and her crew would probably have suffered a similar fate if Capt Detmers had not given the order to abandon ship. He and 320 of his crew managed to get safely clear of the raider before she blew up. The survivors were rescued, and spent the rest of the war as POWs in Australia.

F   **ACTION BETWEEN HSK 8 *KORMORAN* AND HMAS *SYDNEY*, 19 NOVEMBER 1941**

The action took place in the late afternoon of a bright, sunny day in calm seas. The Australian warship had become suspicious when the apparently innocent merchantman turned its stern towards the *Sydney* to present as small a target as possible should *Sydney* open fire. The cruiser closed the distance with *Kormoran* until just off her starboard beam, giving the outgunned raider a perfect opportunity to launch torpedoes and open fire at short range. As soon as the German ship ran up her battle ensign her gunners delivered a storm of fire at *Sydney*'s bridge and forward gun turrets, inflicting massive damage. Battered by both gunfire and torpedoes, *Sydney* lost way as *Kormoran* pulled ahead; but the Australian warship crossed astern of the raider to her port side, and her after turrets managed to score several heavy hits before they too were silenced. The blazing *Sydney* had sustained heavy damage to her engine room, and slowly drifted off as the light failed; a huge explosion was later heard from the *Kormoran*. The raider too was left dead in the water and with fires raging; her crew abandoned ship and were later picked up, the survivors spending the rest of the war in an Australian POW camp.

MICHEL
HSK 9; Schiff 28; Raider H

Specification:			
Built	Danziger Werft, Danzig	Powerplant	2x MAN 8-cylinder diesels
Launched	1939	Top speed	16 knots
Original name	*Bielsko*	Endurance	34,000 n/miles
Length	133m	Armament	6x 15cm guns, 1x 10.5cm, 4x 3.7cm, 4x 2cm; 6x torpedo tubes; 2x Arado Ar196 floatplanes, 1x Schnellboot
Beam	16.8m		
Displacement	4,740 tons	Crew	400

Operational History

The Polish-built freighter *Bielsko* was converted into an auxiliary cruiser at the Deutsche Werft yard at Schichau. She was commissioned into the Kriegsmarine on 7 September 1941, and command was given to Korvettenkapitän Hellmuth von Ruckteschell, formerly captain of the *Widder* in May-October 1940. *Michel* set sail on her first war cruise on 9 March 1942, and despite a determined attack by British destroyers and MTBs as she made the hazardous passage down the English Channel she eventually broke out into the Atlantic on 20 March via Le Havre, St Malo, and La Pallice.

Michel crossed the Equator into the South Atlantic on 5 April 1942, and two weeks later the tanker *Patella* became her first victim. Forced to stop after some well-placed shells knocked out her bridge and radio room, she was sunk with demolition charges. Three days later the American tanker *Connecticut* was sunk with torpedoes fired by the small motor torpedo boat *Esau* which was carried aboard the *Michel*. After refuelling from the tanker *Charlotte Schliemann* on 8 May, *Michel* continued to cruise the South Atlantic, and on the 20th the Norwegian freighter *Kattegat* was sunk with demolition charges.

On 5 June *Michel* intercepted distress signals from the American freighter *George Clymer*, adrift with broken-down engines. Her crew had just managed to effect repairs the next day when the *Esau* raced ahead of the raider and fired two torpedoes into the freighter. Five days later *Michel* encountered the British freighter *Lylepark* and immediately opened fire, rapidly inflicting fatal damage. On 21 June the survivors and other prisoners aboard the raider were transferred to the blockade-runner *Doggerbank*, when *Michel* met up with her and the *Charlotte Schliemann* for refuelling.

HSK 9 *Michel* did not begin her operational career until 1942, and had to fight her way through the English Channel past British destroyers and torpedo boats before breaking out into the Atlantic. (Deutsches U-Boot Museum)

Captain von Ruckteschell's next victim was the British liner *Gloucester Castle*, intercepted on 15 July. Much to the surprise of the German crew this ship, carrying military supplies as well as passengers, rolled over and sank after just a few well-aimed shots had set her on fire. The following day the raider encountered two Allied tankers travelling together. *Michel* attacked the *William F. Humphrey*, hitting her with gunfire and finishing her off with torpedoes, while the *Esau* put two torpedoes into the *Bernhard Hanssen*. Despite this damage the tanker was not stopped, but the *Michel* caught up with her and sank her the following day.

Michel approaches the blockade-runner *Tannenfels* during a rendezvous to resupply the raider; such meetings were the only thing that made cruises of a year and more possible. The auxiliary cruisers would often take such opportunities to transfer their accumulated prisoners. (Deutsches U-Boot Museum)

On 14 August, *Michel* intercepted the freighter *Arabistan* and approached her at full speed; employing his preferred tactic, von Ruckteschell opened fire at point blank range, inflicting such devastating damage that the freighter sank within minutes. *Michel*'s next victim suffered the same fate on 10 September, when the raider closed to almost point blank range with the *American Leader* before opening fire with both guns and torpedoes. The following day another ruinous broadside from close range sank the freighter *Empire Dawn*.

The Indian Ocean and Japan

On 24 September 1942, after refuelling at sea once again, *Michel* headed for the Indian Ocean. It was to be 29 November before she intercepted and sank the freighter *Sawokla* with a combination of *Michel*'s gunfire and torpedoes from *Esau*. On 8 December the raider was herself taken by surprise when the freighter *Eugenie Livanos* suddenly emerged from the cover of a squall. Quickly launching *Esau*, von Ruckteschell began to circle the merchantman, which was soon sunk by both gunfire and torpedoes.

On 26 December 1942, Capt von Ruckteschell received notice that he had been awarded the Oakleaves to his Knight's Cross; *Michel* then began her return voyage to Germany. On 3 January 1943 she intercepted the freighter *Empire March*, which was battered by gunfire and then sunk by torpedoes from both *Michel* and *Esau*. On 9 January the raider captain received new orders: instead of heading home he was to proceed to Japan where, after a fairly uneventful journey, *Michel* moored in Kobe on 2 March 1943, to undergo a refit in the Mitsubishi shipyards.

Here, due to ill health, Capt von Ruckteschell was permitted to relinquish his command to Kapitän zur See Günther Gumprich, stranded in Japan by the accidental loss of his raider *Thor* in Yokohama the previous October. The new captain took *Michel* back to sea on 1 May 1943, heading for the Indian Ocean. There, on 14 June, the raider launched a surprise night attack on the freighter *Höegh Silverdawn* with both gunfire and torpedoes.

Just three days later a large tanker was spotted and followed until nightfall, when *Esau* was launched and sank her with torpedoes. Gumprich then headed back into the Pacific, where targets proved difficult to find.

Michel was the only raider to be destroyed by a US Navy warship, when she was torpedoed and sunk by a US submarine in the approaches to Yokohama in Japan. She had spent nearly a year at sea and had sunk 15 enemy vessels. (Deutsches U-Boot Museum)

Eventually, on 10 September, *Michel* intercepted the tanker *India* near Easter Island. Again the captain shadowed her until nightfall before making his attack; after a few salvoes from *Michel*'s main armament *India*'s tanks were ruptured, spilling her cargo on to the surface of the sea and surrounding her with flames.

Michel's luck finally ran out on 17 October 1943, as she approached Yokohama. The raider was stalked by an American submarine, which loosed a spread of four torpedoes. Two of these hit her; the submarine then passed under the ship, came up and fired a further spread, which blew off her stern. Only 110 of the *Michel*'s crew of 373 were rescued.

 HSK 8 *KORMORAN*

The largest of the auxiliary cruisers began life as another Hansa line ship, the *Steiermark*. Four of her six 15cm guns were mounted each side of her bow and stern behind hinged panels, and the other two were concealed in holds in her deck forward and aft of the main superstructure. Her torpedo tubes were mounted below deck and fired from concealed apertures in the hull. Her two aircraft were carried in the aft hold, and as well as the more typical armament she carried her own motor torpedo boat.

HSK 9 *MICHEL*

When the *Bielsko* of the Gdynia-America line was seized by the Germans it was originally intended that she be converted into a hospital ship, but the decision was later taken to refit her as an auxiliary cruiser. Four of her main guns were mounted either side of the bow and stern behind folding hull plates, the remaining two being concealed in holds on the ship's centreline. The name *Michel* was insisted upon by Korvettenkapitän Helmuth von Ruckteschell against the wishes of the authorities, who did not consider it suitable.

SCHIFF 14, TOGO/CORONEL

The former freighter *Togo* originally served in the Kriegsmarine as a troop transport before being converted into the tenth auxiliary cruiser, as shown here. The name *Coronel* was chosen but never officially bestowed, since she failed in her attempts to break through the English Channel and into the Atlantic in January-February 1943. After her perilous return to Germany she was converted for use as an aircraft direction ship for the Luftwaffe's night fighter defences; compare this view of her with the photograph of her in that role on page 46. After the war she reverted to service as a merchant ship, and survived until the mid 1980s.

LEICHTE SCHNELLBOOT

This type of LS-boat was carried by the *Stier*, *Komet*, *Kormoran* and *Michel*, though only that from *Michel* (which was christened *Esau*) actually entered combat – with some success. These small boats were equipped with an automatic 2cm cannon, and had two rear-firing torpedo tubes.

HSK 8 *KORMORAN*

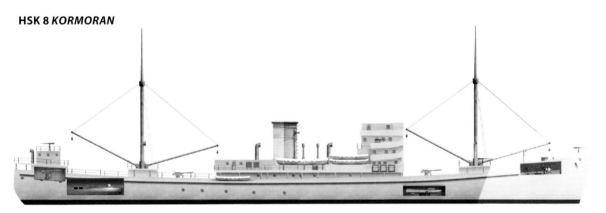

HSK 9 *MICHEL*

SCHIFF 14, *TOGO/ CORONEL*

LEICHTE SCHNELLBOOT

CORONEL
HSK 10; Schiff 14; Raider K

Specification:			
Built	Bremer-Vulkan, Bremen	Powerplant	1x MAN 8-cylinder diesel
Launched	1938	Top speed	16 knots
Original name	*Togo*	Endurance	36,000 n/miles
Length	134m	Armament	6x 15cm guns, 6x 4cm, 8x 2cm; 3x Arado Ar196 floatplanes
Beam	17.9m		
Displacement	5,040 tons	Crew	350

Operational History

As *Togo*, the future *Schiff 14* had already changed her role from a peaceful merchantman into a military vessel in spring 1940, when she was pressed into service as a troop transport for the invasion of Norway, and was damaged by a mine during that operation. After repairs she was formally taken into the Kriegsmarine, and served for a time as a minelayer. In the summer of 1941 she was decommissioned once again and went into the Fijenoord-Werft at Schiedam in occupied Holland for conversion to her new role as an auxiliary cruiser. The work was completed at the Oder-Werke in Stettin in December 1942, at which point she was recommissioned under the command of Kapitän zur See Ernst-Ludwig Thienemann.

After working-up training in the Baltic, *Schiff 14* attempted to break out into the Atlantic via the English Channel on 31 January 1943. (It was traditional that the auxiliary cruisers were given their new names only after reaching their hunting-grounds in the Atlantic.) The operation was dogged with misfortune from the start. While passing through the Heligoland Bight she ran into a storm and had to heave to in order to avoid a number of mines that had torn free from their moorings. A week later, while running through the Channel by night, she ran aground twice on sandbanks off Dunkirk. Fortunately for her the British failed to spot the stranded vessel, but by the time she freed herself for the second time there was no time left to clear the Channel in darkness and she was forced to put into Dunkirk.

The Channel had always been hazardous for German shipping, but by this stage of the war British air power and radar detection had improved markedly since 1940. Leaving port again the following day with a large escort of minesweepers, *Schiff 14* came under fire from British heavy coastal artillery at Dover, and was then attacked by several RAF fighter-bombers. Seriously damaged, she was forced to put into Boulogne, where inspection revealed

The *Togo* was never put to her intended purpose as the auxiliary cruiser *Coronel*, failing to break through the British defences of the English Channel in early 1943. Instead she was employed as part of Germany's anti-aircraft defences, directing fighters towards the incoming streams of Allied bombers. Large radar dishes can clearly be seen in this photo, as well as the domed range-finder housings fore and aft of the funnel. (Deutsches U-Boot Museum)

that several months of repair work would be necessary to make her ocean-worthy again. *Schiff 14* had no option but to return to Germany. During the two days it took for her to prepare for her departure the RAF bombed Boulogne, but the ship escaped any further damage.

On 13 February 1943, *Schiff 14* put to sea again to run the gauntlet of the Dover coastal artillery before putting in at Dunkirk. Here once again attempts were made to eliminate the raider from the air; although she remained unscathed the lock gates were hit, trapping her until repairs could be carried out. A further air raid on 26 February scored hits on her stern, killing several crewmen and causing some flooding but not inflicting enough damage to disable her. Finally, on 27 February, she set sail again with a heavy surface escort, and eventually reached the German port of Cuxhaven on the following day.

Since she had failed to reach the Atlantic, *Schiff 14* never actually received her chosen name of *Coronel*. As *Togo*, she subsequently served as a radar-direction ship for Luftwaffe night-fighters until the closing months of the war, and in January 1945 she was used to evacuate refugees through the Baltic ahead of the Red Army's advance into East Prussia. Following the end of hostilities *Togo* was seized by the British, before being passed on to the USA, who in turn sold the ship to Norway. She eventually returned to private ownership in 1954, and remained in service until November 1984 when, sailing as the *Topeka*, she ran aground and became a total loss.

HANSA

Prior to conversion into an auxiliary cruiser at the Wilton-Fijenoord yard in Rotterdam in 1942, this ship had been used as a target-training vessel for U-boats in the Baltic. Work on conversion was seriously delayed due to crippling material shortages, and when moved to Blohm & Voss in Hamburg for completion of her conversion she was badly damaged in a British air raid during July 1943. The damage was sufficient for conversion work to be abandoned.

Instead *Hansa* was commissioned as a gunnery training ship, and fulfilled that role until February 1944. In the final stages of the war she too was used to evacuate refugees from the Eastern Front down the Baltic, and was finally put out of action when she ran onto a mine on 4 May 1945. Raised after the war, she was taken back into service by her original pre-war owners, eventually being broken up for scrap in 1971.

SUMMARY OF OPERATIONS BY AUXILIARY CRUISERS

Raider	ships sunk	approx tonnage	days at sea
Pinguin	32	154,700	320
Atlantis	22	146,000	601
Orion	16	77,000	510
Michel	15	99,400	354
Thor	12	96,500	328
Kormoran	12	75,400	351
Widder	10	58,600	178
Komet	6	41,000	511
Stier	4	31,000	146
Coronel	0	0	29
Hansa	0	0	0

INDEX

References to illustrations are shown in **bold**.